WOMEN, ABUSE AND TRAUMA THERAPY

An Information Guide for
Women and Their Families

Lori Haskell, EdD, C.Psych.

Centre for Addiction and Mental Health
Centre de toxicomanie et de santé mentale

A Pan American Health Organization /
World Health Organization Collaborating Centre

National Library of Canada Cataloguing in Publication
Haskell, Lori, (date)

Women, Abuse and Trauma Therapy:
An Information Guide for Women and Their Families

ISBN 0-88868-442-8

1. Psychologically abused women—Mental health. 2. Psychologically abused women—Rehabilitation. 3. Post-traumatic stress disorder—Treatment. I. Centre for Addiction and Mental Health. II. Title. III. Series.

RC552.T7H37 2003   616.85'822 C2003-900434-1

Product code: PM033

Printed in Canada
Copyright © 2004 Centre for Addiction and Mental Health

No part of this work may be reproduced or transmitted in any form or by any means electronic or mechanical, including photocopying and recording, or by any information storage and retrieval system without written permission from the publisher—except for a brief quotation (not to exceed 200 words) in a review or professional work.

For information on other Centre for Addiction and Mental Health resource materials or to place an order, please contact:
Marketing and Sales Services
Centre for Addiction and Mental Health
33 Russell Street
Toronto, ON M5S 2S1
Canada

Tel.: 1 800 661-1111 or 416 595-6059 in Toronto
E-mail: marketing@camh.net

Web site: www.camh.net

Disponible en français sous le titre *Les femmes, la violence et le traitement des traumatismes : Guide d'information à l'intention des femmes et de leur famille*

This guide was produced by the following:

DEVELOPMENT
Julia Greenbaum, CAMH

DESIGN
Nancy Leung, CAMH

EDITORIAL
Susan Morton Stewart,
Colborne Communications

PRINT PRODUCTION
Chris Harris, CAMH

MARKETING
Rosalicia Rondon, CAMH

CONTENTS

Introduction v

1 Understanding Psychological Trauma 1

2 A Trauma Model for Therapy 6

3 The Therapeutic Relationship 9

4 Choosing a Therapist 15

5 Stages of Trauma Therapy 18

6 Treatment Approaches 23

7 How to Assess Your Therapist 27

8 How Do I Know If My Therapy Is Helping? 29

9 Family and Friends 31

10 Getting Access to Services 36

11 The Strength of Survivors 38

Suggested Readings 39

Glossary 43

ACKNOWLEDGMENTS

AUTHOR
Lori Haskell EdD, C.Psych.

PROJECT MANAGER
Julia Greenbaum

RESEARCHER
Diana Ballon

CONSULTANT
Melanie Randall (Centre for Research on Violence against Women and Children, University of Western Ontario, London, Ontario)

We acknowledge the following Centre for Addiction and Mental Health staff for their feedback on earlier versions of this guide:
Karen Belfontaine (Mood and Anxiety Program)
Jennifer Chambers (Client Empowerment Council)
Barb Dorian (Psychological Trauma Program)
Ursula Kasperowski (Personality Disorder Service)
Betty Miller (Family Empowerment Council)
Ellie Munn (Community Programs)
Teresa Naseba Marsh (Substance Abuse Program for African Canadian and Caribbean Youth)
Mary Quartarone (Education and Publishing)

We extend our gratitude to the following women who, along with others who wish to remain anonymous, provided helpful feedback on an earlier draft of this guide:
Sandi Bell of EMPOWWORD Inc.
Darlene Buligan
Karyn Hand
Svetlana Iankilevitch
Cherie Lynn Knight
Debbie Moon
Joan Piscopo
Heather Riley
Lynn Wright

INTRODUCTION

Who Should Read This Guide, and Why?

This guide is for women who are in therapy, or who are looking for a therapist, to help them deal with the long-term effects of prolonged or repeated experiences of abuse and violence. It is also for family members and friends who want to understand and support a woman who is going through trauma therapy. Therapists may also find it useful as a resource to give to clients or to use themselves.

For many women, choosing to go into therapy to deal with a past traumatic event or a series of traumatic events is a huge step. It can take a lot of time, money and emotional energy. While a lot of trauma information is available to professionals, there is not much general information that women can use to help them understand their trauma responses and to get the most out of their trauma therapy.

This guide gives information about the therapeutic process and what to expect from one-on-one trauma therapy. Even though the focus of this guide is on individual counselling rather than group therapy, most of the material is also applicable to trauma treatment carried out in the context of a group.

This information helps women feel more confident about seeking help. It helps women gain control over the healing process so they can:

- know what to expect from therapy
- choose the best therapy and therapist for themselves.

If you do not know whether trauma therapy is right for you, see Section 2, "A Trauma Model for Therapy," or read the CAMH brochure *Women: What Do These Signs Have in Common?*

This guide will also help you:

- understand psychological trauma, post-traumatic stress and common responses to trauma
- learn about different types of therapy for abuse-related trauma
- learn what a trauma approach to therapy is and what to expect from trauma therapy
- understand the client/therapist relationship and how to assess your therapist
- know what to expect from trauma therapy at different stages of therapy
- know if the therapy is working
- get support from family and friends.

1 UNDERSTANDING PSYCHOLOGICAL TRAUMA

What Is Abuse-Related Trauma?

This guide discusses trauma resulting from abuse, often called "abuse-related trauma."

Abuse-related trauma can develop after someone has been sexually or physically abused and/or emotionally abused or neglected, usually in childhood. The abuser is often an older family member or a close family friend or relative. Women who experience trauma as adults are most often those who felt helpless and trapped by abuse as children.

Trauma can change the way a person develops, emotionally and psychologically. This is because traumatic events can disrupt your emotions, memory, consciousness and sense of self. Trauma can affect your relationships and your **attachment** to others. It can change the way your brain and body work.

Whether an event is considered traumatic is based on a woman's own experience. A "traumatic event" (incident that causes trauma) may overwhelm a woman's ability to cope. She may feel as though she is "going crazy." Many abused women feel distressed, afraid and helpless.

Traumatic events come in many forms, and people cope with them in different ways, but there are some patterns in the ways people respond to abuse. These patterns depend on:

- the person's age at the time of the abuse
- the abuse survivor's relationship to the person who abused her
- whether the abuse happened once or was repeated over time.

What Is Post-Traumatic Stress?

Life-threatening or overwhelming events such as car accidents, natural disasters, war, or sexual or physical assault may lead to post-traumatic stress. **Post-traumatic stress** can develop when a person experiences the effects of a traumatic event long after the event is over. Sometimes these negative effects can last for many years.

Post-traumatic stress is a *normal* response to extreme harm.

Women who experience post-traumatic stress may not think their abuse experiences were very serious. Many women cope with the devastation by minimizing the effects of the abuse on their lives, making the abuse seem less important.

DIFFERENT KINDS OF POST-TRAUMATIC STRESS— SIMPLE AND COMPLEX

Simple post-traumatic stress results from a one-time incident, such as a rape or serious car accident. It is different from complex post-traumatic stress.

Complex post-traumatic stress usually develops if the abuse:

- happened over a long period of time
- was repeated many times
- was committed by the person's caregivers
- happened early in life, especially if the child experienced emotional neglect or poor attachment in his or her family.

Complex post-traumatic stress can also develop in adulthood, when abuse happens over a long time (for example, when a woman is battered by her partner over a number of years).

People who have experienced severe abuse can have complex post-traumatic stress without having simple post-traumatic stress. But generally, they have both.

What Are the Most Common Responses to Trauma?

Women respond to traumatic events in different ways. They may:

- have intense emotions, but not realize what causes them
- remember the traumatic event, but not feel anything
- feel suddenly alert and panicky
- be constantly vigilant and irritable, and not know why
- feel numb and empty.

SIMPLE POST-TRAUMATIC STRESS RESPONSES

Simple post-traumatic responses usually happen after one traumatic event. The person may:

- have nightmares or **flashbacks** about the traumatic event (a flashback is a sudden, disruptive and vivid re-experiencing of a traumatic event)
- avoid things that remind her of the event
- feel numb
- spend less time with family and friends
- lose interest in everyday activities
- be always on guard or alert to danger.

COMPLEX POST-TRAUMATIC STRESS RESPONSES

Responses to complex post-traumatic stress may include:

- having general feelings of despair
- feeling that life is meaningless or that you are worthless
- experiencing **depression**
- feeling unexplained shame or guilt
- having problems trusting or being close to others
- being prone to emotional outbursts and impulsiveness
- having difficulty feeling calm or relaxed
- having long-term problems with sleeping
- not feeling entitled to your own feelings, opinions or wishes
- feeling that you don't deserve success and happiness.

To cope with painful feelings, many women:

- develop an **eating disorder**
- misuse alcohol or other drugs
- self-harm by cutting or burning themselves
- spend less time with others because it feels safer to be alone
- try to please others so they don't get angry, disappointed or hurt.

These ways of coping often make women feel more isolated and depressed, and can increase anxiety and sleeping problems.

These behaviours may help women cope with some painful feelings for a while. But, over time, they become less effective. Women usually start therapy when they find they can't cope any longer with the problems in their relationships or in everyday life. For example, they may have trouble sleeping, or find that their work is overwhelming or that parenting is too stressful.

SUBSTANCE USE, DEPRESSION, EATING DISORDERS AND OTHER PROBLEMS

Many people coping with trauma have other problems, such as substance use, depression or an eating disorder. These problems are often a response to the trauma. Trauma therapy can help with these kinds of problems. But you may also want to get other help at the same time, such as by joining a support group.

Understanding Yourself with Empathy and Respect

Many survivors of childhood abuse and neglect grew up in homes where they were criticized, not listened to and blamed for many of the hurtful things that were done to them.

As a result, many survivors still blame themselves. They may not trust others. They may believe that others will not treat them respectfully or understand their feelings.

The goal of therapy is to help you heal by listening to you respectfully and with empathy and care. Survivors learn to have empathy for themselves both by being treated respectfully and by learning about normal responses to trauma. Learning that many of the behaviours that you developed are normal reactions to overwhelming experiences will help you feel less shame and responsibility for what you have experienced.

2. A TRAUMA MODEL FOR THERAPY

Traditional therapy often does not:

- link trauma to childhood abuse and neglect
- consider the social conditions of women's lives
- view the ways women cope as normal responses to abnormal events.

As a result, many women who have post-traumatic stress have not received effective help.

THE TRAUMA THERAPY MODEL

People who have survived abuse are best helped by therapy that works from an understanding of how abuse and neglect, especially in childhood, affect the way people think, feel, behave and relate to others.

An effective **trauma therapy model** should also make links between trauma and social inequalities, such as sexism, racism and poverty in women's lives.

DEVELOPING A RELATIONSHIP OF COLLABORATION
In the trauma therapy model, therapy needs to happen in a relationship of **collaboration**. This means that clients are not viewed as people being treated for an illness. Instead, they are viewed as partners in healing—they share responsibility with the therapist for their own care.

UNDERSTANDING PROBLEMS AS "RESPONSES"
A trauma therapy model considers whether individual problems are the result of abuse and neglect. It understands that:

- Women's ways of coping are normal responses to overwhelming experiences.

- Women's emotional problems often develop in a context of abuse and ongoing stress (rather than viewing these problems as symptoms of something that is wrong with the woman).

RECOGNIZING SOCIAL INEQUALITY

An effective trauma therapy model should also recognize that individual problems can be made worse by the social conditions of women's lives. Some mental health providers do not fully understand the social and psychological factors that shape women's choices and responses. For instance, they often do not take into account that women's problems may be partly caused or intensified by ongoing racism, sexism, homophobia and conditions of poverty. These conditions are part of many women's everyday lives, and can worsen feelings women already have of being unsafe and disempowered.

RECOGNIZING THE SEVERITY OF TRAUMA

Trauma therapists also need to recognize that:

- Suffering from abuse is severe and often lasts for years, even after the abuse has ended.
- Survivors often feel ashamed, and minimize how much they have been hurt by these harmful experiences.

What to Expect from Abuse-Related Trauma Therapy

If you know what to expect from therapy, you may feel safer and more confident about your treatment. If you understand how therapy works, you will also know if you are not getting the help you need. Then you can decide if you need to change therapists.

To help you best, a therapist will need to learn a lot about your life. Your therapist will ask questions such as:

- How long do you remember feeling the way you do?
- What do you do when you feel this way?
- What therapies or medications have you already tried?

Therapy will help you connect to emotions you have blocked out of your life for years. This means you will have both painful and good feelings. To heal, you may sometimes feel worse before you begin to feel better. Therapy may take many years to complete.

Women have many different responses to memories of their abuse (e.g., nightmares, sleep disturbances, **dissociation**, depression, humiliation, anger, self-hatred). Effective therapy aims to help you remember your experiences and face your feelings with the aid of new coping strategies and resources. Although you have to face the pain, you do it using new internal resources (e.g., safe place imagery, self soothing) and increased external resources (e.g., support from friends or family, a safe place to live).

Often, people in therapy are in a hurry to "get better." But if you try to move too quickly in therapy, you can become overwhelmed. For example, you may start to explore your painful experiences before you are ready. Your therapist needs to teach you about the possible effects of moving too quickly. You need to work with your therapist to set a pace for therapy.

3 THE THERAPEUTIC RELATIONSHIP

The goals for your relationship with your therapist are to:

- develop a "collaborative alliance" (or connection)
- learn to set boundaries
- understand yourself with empathy and respect.

Developing a Collaborative Alliance

A **collaborative alliance** is the positive connection you make with your therapist. It is important to develop an alliance with your therapist, because a lot of the distress women experience is related to the way they were hurt in a close relationship.

Many abuse survivors find that the relationship with a therapist makes them anxious. People often feel betrayed, powerless and taken advantage of when someone they trust abuses them. When this happens, many women begin to believe that others can't be trusted or relied on for support. So relationships with others, especially relationships with people who are in a position of power, or with people you rely on, may seem dangerous and threatening.

Many abuse survivors start therapy expecting that their relationship with the therapist will have dangers similar to those in the relationship with the person who abused them. This is not surprising. In the abuse survivor/therapist relationship, the therapist is in a position of power, and the survivor feels less powerful. Because of this power, survivors may find it hard to talk about their feelings and reactions to trauma, about which they may feel shame, anger, fear or anxiety.

People need to heal within a relationship in order to see relationships as positive and safe. Learning to trust and feel safe with a therapist helps people form relationship skills. This helps them build more meaningful and respectful connections with others.

REACTIONS YOU MAY HAVE TO YOUR THERAPIST

Abuse survivors have learned different ways to avoid and negotiate relationships to stay safe from more abuse or to protect themselves from being abandoned or neglected. You may find yourself using some of these methods in your relationship with your therapist.

- You may try to keep your relationship with your therapist safe by going along with what your therapist wants or says. At the same time, you may ignore your own thoughts, feelings and needs.
- You may test your therapist's ability to deal with your thoughts and feelings by only telling the therapist a tiny amount of what you really think or feel.
- You may try to tell your therapist interesting stories so you don't have to talk about your painful feelings.
- You may try to please your therapist by bringing in gifts or asking questions about the therapist, because you don't feel your needs are important to others.

Your therapist should be trained to understand the ways you protect yourself. She or he shouldn't punish you, reject you or withdraw from you. Instead, you should expect guidance, suggestions and directions from your therapist. Your therapist should encourage you to discuss only the things that you feel able to talk about.

It is normal to have different reactions to the therapist at different times during your therapy—you may:

- feel a positive connection
- feel nervous because you need someone's help
- feel that you are valued and cared for
- feel too vulnerable to reveal yourself.

Your relationship with your therapist is, in some important ways, like any other relationship. You may have misunderstandings; you may feel disappointed, let down or even angry.

Many people don't realize before they start therapy that the relationship with their therapist is very important. For some people, it is the first time they have truly felt safe and listened to. It is not unusual for therapy clients (not just abuse survivors) to feel that they are loved by their therapist. This is difficult for some people, because the positive experiences with their therapist may bring up many strong feelings. These feelings can range from fear of being dependent on the therapist to wanting the therapist to meet your unfulfilled needs.

There is nothing wrong with having these feelings—they are normal. It is the therapist's responsibility to give you a safe and predictable relationship in which to explore these feelings, while always staying inside the boundaries of the relationship.

With a respectful and trustworthy therapist, abuse survivors can work through the stressful feelings that may arise during therapy. This is because the issues that come up between client and therapist often are similar to problems in the survivor's other relationships. Like all relationships, the therapeutic relationship will have difficulties and disagreements. This does *not* mean that the relationship is a failure. Instead, looking at the problems in the safety of the therapeutic relationship will give you feedback as you practise relating to others. This will help you to have more satisfying relationships outside of therapy.

If you feel uncomfortable with your therapist, it's important to discuss your concerns with him or her. While you have the right to end your therapy at any time, it is useful to talk about the conflict and check out your concerns, in case there has been any misunderstanding or misinterpretation that can be worked through. Many therapists will ask you to let them know if you feel misunderstood. At other times your therapist may realize that he or she made a mistake and will talk about it with you. For example, a therapist might not understand the importance of something you said, or might respond with impatience instead of understanding.

For many survivors, an important part of therapy is changing from seeing people as either good or bad (a way of protecting yourself, or what is called a "self-protective stance"). Instead, you learn that everyone has limitations and can make mistakes. Most therapists believe it is important to talk about any concerns you have in your life, as well as concerns you have about your therapy.

Learning to Set Boundaries

Women who have had their physical and emotional boundaries violated over and over will need to learn how to set boundaries. Setting boundaries is a difficult psychological task, but is important in developing healthy relationships.

what are boundaries?

Boundaries define your personal space and limits, and let others know how to relate to you.

Physical boundaries are the limits you place around bodily contact, especially in sexual situations. These kinds of boundaries allow you to protect your personal space. For example, many women find it helpful to set limits on the kind of sexual touch they are comfortable with, such as asking their romantic partners not to touch them from behind, especially when they are not expecting it.

Emotional boundaries protect your feelings and thoughts and your right to experience and express what you think or feel. For example, if someone asks you a personal question that you are not comfortable answering, you set a boundary by saying, "I am not really comfortable with that question," or "What you have asked me is my private business."

Finding the right distance between two people emotionally and physically is the key to setting safe boundaries. Many survivors become too involved with friends or intimate partners, making themselves and others uncomfortable. Other abuse survivors, in an effort to protect themselves, may remain too distant and are unable to make strong friendships or intimacies.

With the help of a skilled therapist, you can observe how you set boundaries and learn how to protect yourself more effectively, both physically and emotionally.

TYPES OF BOUNDARIES

Boundaries are important in therapy for the benefit and protection of both you and the therapist. Most boundaries are worked out between you and your therapist. Some of the boundaries are laws that the therapist has to follow, for example, a therapist cannot have a sexual relationship with a client.

The more predictable and consistent the boundaries are, the safer you will feel. You and your therapist will probably talk about some of the following boundaries.

Physical closeness
Therapists should talk with you about boundaries for touching. Some therapists have firm rules that they never touch their clients, while other therapists may use touch in therapy to help ground or comfort their clients. Your therapist should always ask before touching you.

Therapist revealing personal information
Therapists should always let clients know what information they will discuss about themselves.

Client disclosing information
Part of the safety of therapy is that you know that your therapist respects the pace you want to set for discussing painful or personal issues in your life. If you are not ready to deal with certain issues, you don't have to. Learning to express your personal limits in therapy, with the help of your therapist, is how you learn to set emotional boundaries.

Your therapist should also work with you to look back over situations where you have felt uncomfortable or frightened with others, so that you can learn from these situations. An important part of self-care is being able to anticipate your future needs in setting boundaries.

Therapist accessibility
Your therapist should talk with you about whether she or he is available to speak to you on the phone between sessions, and what to do in case of an emergency.

A therapist should not start a **dual relationship**. As your therapist, he or she can't also be your friend or someone you socialize with, or someone who provides any other service to you. For example, if you receive trauma therapy from your medical doctor, that doctor should refer you to another doctor for your physical examinations. This should be done before the therapy begins.

Behavioural limits
Your therapist will need you to agree to control aggressive or violent behaviour in the treatment setting. You will also need to agree not to drink or use recreational drugs before therapy sessions.

Rules for therapy
The therapist should talk with you about the rules for therapy. For example, the therapist must maintain confidentiality, but must report information to the authorities if you inform him or her of any current abuse of children in your life. Other rules usually include that you keep appointments and cancel or reschedule your appointments with enough notice. Most therapists will talk with you about how much you need to pay for therapy and when and how you make your payments.

4 CHOOSING A THERAPIST

THINGS TO CONSIDER WHEN LOOKING FOR A THERAPIST

Therapy for abuse-related trauma is usually a long-term commitment. The first abuse you suffered was most likely in your childhood. You may have spent many years trying to deal with the pain of an abusive experience. So, taking the time to find a therapist you're comfortable with is very important.

Anyone can call himself or herself a "psychotherapist," "therapist" or "counsellor" and advertise his or her services without having any special training. There is no one to regulate these types of therapists or respond to any complaints about them.

It is important to find out what kind of qualifications a therapist has before you agree to start therapy with her or him. Good therapists should want to explain to you where they were educated and if they have any special training in various areas of therapy. A professional therapist may be a psychologist, a social worker or a psychiatrist. Your therapist should at least have a university degree in a clinical counselling field at a graduate level, from a recognized university.

It is very important to find a professional with specialized training in trauma therapy, and experience working with women who have been abused.

Most therapists who offer trauma treatment have completed specialized education and courses in post-traumatic stress. This extra training can be in the form of programs offered at universities, hospital- or community-based workshops, professional training programs, seminars and conferences.

If you feel more comfortable with a therapist who is the same gender, sexual orientation or ethnic background as you, then consider this before you start looking for a therapist. When getting a referral to a trauma therapist, try to get more than one name, and get on several waiting lists, if necessary. It is usually worth waiting to work with a mental health professional with specific training and skills necessary for trauma treatment.

Questions to Ask Potential Therapists

Take this list of questions with you when you are interviewing therapists. Write down the answers in a notebook. A professional therapist should be happy to answer all of these questions. Also notice *how* the therapist responds to your questions: are you comfortable with the therapist's manner?

QUESTIONS ABOUT QUALIFICATIONS AND PROFESSIONAL EXPERIENCE

- What are your qualifications?
- Do you belong to a recognized professional organization?
- How long have you been providing therapy?
- What experience do you have in treating abuse-related trauma?
- How do you approach treatment for simple post-traumatic stress?
- How do you approach treatment for complex post-traumatic stress?

QUESTIONS ABOUT THE THERAPIST'S PRACTICE

- What do you charge for the therapy you provide?
- Are you covered by OHIP or by third-party insurance?
- Do you have a sliding scale (people pay what they can afford for the therapy)?
- How long are sessions?
- When and how do you bill?
- What is your policy about cancellations or missed sessions?
- What are your rules about phone calls between sessions or contact outside of therapy?
- What is your policy about physical contact with clients?
- What happens if you go on vacation or take time off?

OTHER IMPORTANT QUESTIONS

- Have you ever had a formal complaint made against you?
- Have you ever been disciplined or censured (official disapproval) by a professional organization?
- Do you think we can work together and that you can help me?
- Is there anything else I need to know about your services?

Questions to Ask Yourself

After interviewing the potential therapist, ask yourself the following questions:

- Did the therapist answer openly and without being defensive?
- Did the therapist encourage my questions?
- Did the therapist treat me and my questions with respect?
- Did the therapist answer the questions in a way that I could understand?
- Was the therapist's approach to therapy similar to what this guide describes?
- Do I think the therapist has experience and qualifications to do this work?
- Could I imagine talking to this person about personal issues?
- Can I afford this therapy?

5 STAGES OF TRAUMA THERAPY

THE TRAUMA THERAPY MODEL: THREE STAGES OF TREATMENT

Most therapy professionals agree that the standard and best approach for working with trauma survivors should follow these three stages:

1. stabilizing and managing responses
2. processing and grieving traumatic memories
3. reconnecting with the world.

Abuse survivors need to find ways to manage their reactions to trauma before they can start to look at the causes of the trauma. This is the first stage of therapy and is normally the longest. Some abuse survivors may decide to stop therapy after this step.

In the second stage, survivors begin to explore their childhood traumatic memories. Even after survivors move to the second stage of trauma treatment, they often still need to return to some of the skills that they learn in the first stage of treatment.

In fact, survivors will often return to stage one of the therapy during stages two and three. This is natural and you shouldn't see it as a step back. If you try to complete stage two before completing stage one, you will not be prepared for the emotions that come with stage two. This may be harmful.

The third and final stage of trauma treatment begins after the traumatic memories have been processed. This stage deals with any issues relating to daily life, relationships and being connected with the world.

First Stage

The first stage of trauma therapy will teach you about trauma and therapy. In this stage, you will create more effective strategies to manage the effects of trauma on your life (sometimes called "symptoms"). These new skills and knowledge should help you to feel more stable and better able to function in your life.

The first stage of trauma treatment does not involve looking at or dealing with early experiences of abuse. However, it's important for the abuse survivor to acknowledge any experience of abuse or neglect. That way the therapist and client can begin a process of helping the client understand how the past affects the present.

The three key tasks of first stage trauma treatment are: establishing safety, psychoeducation and managing trauma responses.

ESTABLISHING SAFETY

The first step of stage one is for the therapist to address any safety issues in your life, including:

- finding safe housing (if you are living with someone who is emotionally, physically or sexually abusive)
- setting safety rules with the therapist
- checking to see if you are actively suicidal or need protection from harming yourself
- arranging a referral to a physician to check for any medical conditions (such as a thyroid problem) that could be making your physical responses worse, and to assess the need for medication, should you have depression, anxiety and fatigue
- making a treatment plan that helps you with any problems of alcohol or other drugs.

PSYCHOEDUCATION

Much of the focus in the first stage of trauma therapy is on psychoeducation. You learn how trauma affects how you think, feel and act. You may also learn about flashbacks, dissociation or numbing.

MANAGING TRAUMA RESPONSES

The first step in managing your traumatic stress responses will be for you and the therapist to decide which trauma responses are the most painful and which interfere most in your everyday life. You can then work together to rank your responses from those that cause you the most problems to those that hurt you the least.

The therapist should use various ways to help you manage your traumatic stress responses and adaptations. These strategies will help you feel stronger and better able to cope, and find ways to care for yourself. While you may not stop or get rid of all your negative responses, these strategies should help you to control them better.

It is important to understand that the coping behaviours you developed to deal with traumatic stress (such as the use of alcohol or other drugs to block the pain) are typical behaviours that people use. These coping behaviours may temporarily help you avoid painful, disturbing feelings or thoughts but they will also interfere with your healing.

The therapist should explain the purpose of the techniques and strategies you learn about in therapy, so that you understand them fully and can practise them on your own.

Second Stage

The second, or middle, stage of trauma therapy involves looking at past experiences of trauma. It explores how the trauma has affected you in the past and how it continues to affect you.

PROCESSING AND GRIEVING TRAUMATIC MEMORIES

Processing traumatic experiences can be difficult and requires special methods. The most effective methods for dealing with traumatic memories are:

- cognitive-behavioural therapy (CBT)
- eye movement desensitization reprocessing therapy (EMDR)
- body-psychotherapy and Sensorimotor Psychotherapy.

These methods are all explained in Section 6, "Treatment Approaches" (below). With both CBT techniques and EMDR techniques, survivors are asked to remember all aspects of the incident(s) as vividly as possible, including aspects that involve the senses (sight, smell, touch, hearing).

Many survivors instinctively avoid memories, thoughts and feelings related to the abuse they suffered, but avoiding these things prolongs the trauma responses and prevents survivors from getting over trauma-related difficulties.

Facing painful experiences instead of avoiding them lets survivors process the traumatic experience, and then the pain and anxiety will gradually lessen. Many women find that they have more intense feelings and reactions to the abuse when they are confronting their memories. However, you should *not* be in a constant state of crisis. If this happens, the therapy should return to the first stage of helping you feel more stable and able to manage your reactions.

Third Stage

The third and last stage of trauma therapy involves addressing any remaining difficulties in your life, as well as working on ways to connect fully in your relationships with others.

RECONNECTING WITH THE WORLD

The third, or final, stage is about dealing with the issues of daily life for survivors who are doing well, but who are still struggling with certain issues.

For example, you may feel pretty good, but have a hard time reconnecting with friends and family, have trouble finding work you enjoy, find it difficult to get involved in activities you used to enjoy or struggle to maintain healthy relationships.

As in stage two, survivors will continue to change the way that they look at their lives. They will continue to find new meaning and new ways to understand the past, and bring optimism, hope, spirituality and creativity to their future.

While clients will have already dealt with the trauma, effects of the abuse may still come up in new situations they are dealing with in their lives. This is normal and not uncommon.

6 TREATMENT APPROACHES

The trauma therapy model outlines the stages of therapy and the steps that happen in each stage. But different therapists will use different treatment approaches within the model to help you deal with the trauma.

In order to understand what to expect at every stage of the trauma therapy model, you need to know the range of therapeutic approaches your therapist may use. The following example shows how the trauma therapy model can include different approaches to working with clients.

A trauma abuse survivor tells her therapist that she is very anxious and can't sleep. The trauma therapy model says that her anxiety needs to be dealt with and managed before other issues in her life are looked at. The techniques used to help her with her anxiety and sleeplessness will differ depending on what the therapist has been trained in.

One therapist may use a treatment approach called **cognitive-behavioural therapy** (CBT). Another therapist may use other approaches, such as **eye movement desensitization reprocessing** (EMDR), **hypnotherapy** or **guided imagery**. These aim to help the woman feel calmer and less overwhelmed by her emotions. A psychiatrist may prescribe medications to help her sleep and reduce her anxiety. These treatment approaches are all described below and in the glossary.

Most skilled therapists are trained in several different types of treatment, which they may use in combination or alone. But all treatment approaches should follow the stages of the trauma therapy model. Effective therapists will adapt the different treatment approaches to suit you best.

Here is a brief description of the main therapeutic approaches:

PSYCHOEDUCATION

Psychoeducation teaches abuse survivors about different psychological processes and their effects. For example, the therapist may explain that what you are feeling and doing is typical of reactions that other survivors also describe; after learning that your feelings are normal, you may begin to feel less isolated or "crazy." Your therapist may also explain the effects of trauma in both the short term and long term, and how trauma can affect your body, your emotions and how you develop.

The therapist may also give you information about abuse and neglect.

All of the information isn't given at one time, but throughout your therapy, depending on what you are discussing and dealing with at the time.

COGNITIVE-BEHAVIOURAL THERAPY

Cognitive-behavioural therapy (CBT) focuses on helping the client become aware of how thoughts, attitudes, expectations and beliefs can contribute to feelings of unhappiness. The client learns how certain beliefs, which may have been developed in the past to deal with difficult or painful experiences, are no longer helpful or true in the current situation. The client can then try to change the behaviours, thoughts and beliefs that are no longer helpful.

Often, CBT involves homework or written exercises. For instance, the client may do various written exercises in which she explores the accuracy of certain negative beliefs (e.g., the mistaken belief that she was somehow responsible for her own abuse) by questioning or challenging evidence to support her perspective.

CBT can also involve what is called "exposure techniques." This is particularly helpful for people with simple post-traumatic stress; that is, those who have been traumatized by a single event. **Exposure therapy** involves gradually exposing the person to the feared situation until she becomes desensitized, or no longer reactive to what originally created so much fear.

CBT can also involve helping the client to develop coping strategies to reduce her anxiety. This may include breathing retraining, relaxation and imagery or visualization exercises.

Eye Movement Desensitization Reprocessing

Eye movement desensitization reprocessing (EMDR) is a new psychotherapy used to treat responses to traumatic experiences, such as anxiety, guilt, depression, panic, sleep disturbance and flashbacks. EMDR is not a complete therapy system, but is a technique that can be used within a therapeutic approach to treat trauma.

The idea behind EMDR is that people who have experienced trauma or other difficult experiences have stored memories without adequately processing them. EMDR is a therapeutic approach that accelerates the integration of traumatic memories. EMDR stimulates the brain's natural information processing mechanisms, allowing the "frozen" traumatic information to be processed normally and become integrated.

Traumatic memories are believed to be "locked" in the nervous system. As a result, various triggers can cause the person to re-experience the original traumatic images, sensations and thoughts at a later time.

Because the left hemisphere (section) of the brain helps to create meaning and organize memories, left hemisphere processes can help relieve distress. However, traumatic memories are believed to be stored in the right hemisphere and so cannot be processed by left hemisphere processes.

Side-to-side stimulation (for example, through eye movements) seems to unlock memories by allowing the processing of information between the right and left hemispheres of the brain. In this way the person processes the traumatic memory, which had been "locked" into one side of the brain, and balance is restored. This process is thought to be similar to what happens during dreaming and REM sleep.

Note: EMDR can only be done by a properly trained clinician and is used as part of a larger treatment plan.

Medication

Many people with post-traumatic stress find that medication gives them relief from sleeplessness, depression, panic attacks and other reactions. Psychologists, social workers and other non–medically trained therapists cannot prescribe medication. So if you are considering medication, you will need to be referred to a medical doctor or psychiatrist. The doctor should be trained in understanding post-traumatic stress as well as in psychotropic drugs (the medications used to treat mental health issues). Medication can help you manage some of the effects of trauma. But it is not a complete solution, and is best used along with therapy.

Body-Psychotherapy

Trauma affects the body and the mind, and a good therapy method should deal with both. **Body-psychotherapy** is a form of therapy that deals with physiological reactions to trauma. Some body techniques do not involve touch, and are suited to people who are uncomfortable with being touched in therapy.

Sensorimotor Psychotherapy is a type of body-psychotherapy that helps survivors deal with disturbing bodily reactions. It can help you manage and disconnect physical feelings from trauma-based emotions. Sensorimotor Psychotherapy uses the body (rather than thoughts or feelings) as the main way to deal with trauma. In turn, this helps emotional and mental well-being.

Therapists using this technique will sometimes touch clients, but only when clients give consent.

7 HOW TO ASSESS YOUR THERAPIST

Your relationship with your therapist is very important. If you are not comfortable with the way that your therapist is addressing your issues, you can ask for a referral to (or a consultation with) another therapist or mental health professional. Alternatively, you can bring in this guide and go through it with your therapist, explaining what you were expecting from therapy.

You can decide if the treatment you are getting is helpful or appropriate by asking yourself the following questions.

COMMUNICATION
- Do you feel respected and validated by your therapist?
- Is the therapist working collaboratively with you as a partner, or is the therapist imposing his or her own suggestions on you? (For example, do you work with your therapist to identify the central concerns?)
- Does your therapist view you as the expert on your own life?
- Does your therapist respond with warmth and empathy?
- Does your therapist believe that you can gain control over your responses?
- Does your therapist explain the process of therapy, review your experience with you, and see if it is helping?
- Do you feel that your therapist actively talks with you and gives you feedback (for example, does your therapist explain the therapy and ask whether it is helping you)?
- Does your therapist have clear rules (for example, keeping the appointment time, not missing appointments, not starting late, not rescheduling without an explanation, not running over time)?

SUPPORT
- Does the therapist help you see your strengths and the effective ways that you have coped with your trauma? (For example, does your therapist describe "symptoms and problems" as understandable ways that you have adapted and coped?)

- Does your therapist help you with your trauma responses (for example, help to "ground" you when you feel overwhelmed, or bring you back to the present so that you can separate the past abuse from your current circumstance)?
- Does your therapist "check in" with you to see how you have been between sessions? (For example, does she or he ask questions like: "How were you after last session?"; "Were you able to sleep?"; "Is this working?"; etc.)
- Does your therapist encourage you to be involved in different activities, meet with friends, explore other outlets to express emotions (artistic, physical, spiritual)?
- Does your therapist ask you about other supports in your life and encourage you to be involved in other activities (for example, paid/volunteer work, classes, meeting up with friends)?

INFORMATION

- Does your therapist explain how trauma or long-term stress can cause changes to the body, mind and emotions?
- Has your therapist asked you to have a full medical examination to make sure that you do not have any medical problems that could be adding to feelings of tension or discomfort in your body?
- Does your therapist ask you about depression, sleep problems or suicidal feelings? If you have difficulties with any of the above, has the therapist suggested that you consult with a psychiatrist or medical doctor trained in trauma treatment to discuss medication?

THERAPIST SKILLS

- Does your therapist use a variety of specialized skills and techniques that address your specific needs?
- If your therapist does not have a specific skill or knowledge, has she or he suggested a referral?

8 HOW DO I KNOW IF MY THERAPY IS HELPING?

It is very important to develop a trusting relationship with a therapist, and to feel comfortable and respected. However, this is only part of the therapy.

You may find that once you start therapy, you feel worse at first, but this does *not* mean the therapy isn't working. However, some women find that they are always in a state of crisis. Their therapists may not have helped them develop ways to cope with their overwhelming emotions. If this is true for you, the therapy is probably moving too quickly. Or your therapist may be getting you to think and talk about the traumatic events before you are ready.

You'll know if the therapy is working by asking yourself the following questions.

INCREASED ABILITY TO SOOTHE YOURSELF
- Are you better able to understand, recognize and name your traumatic responses and the things that can **trigger** these responses?
- Are you feeling more content in your life?
- Are you getting upset less often?
- If you get upset, do you think that you will be able to take care of yourself?
- If you get upset, can you recognize that something from the past has affected the present?

UNDERSTANDING YOURSELF
- Do you have more insight about the events in your life and how they affected you?
- Do you know what you are working on in therapy, and do you have clear goals in therapy?
- Can you see that some ways of coping that once helped are now causing problems?
- Do you have a better understanding of the behaviours you developed as a means to cope and adapt to life?

POSITIVE COPING

- Are you able to set limits and boundaries with people? Do you feel more in control of your own life?
- Have you been able to develop more positive and effective ways of coping?
- Do you have a safety plan? For example, if you are re-experiencing the abuse through flashbacks or nightmares, do you have a plan that includes methods to soothe yourself, techniques to help you separate the past from the present, or a list of names of friends or supports to call?
- Can you apply the skills and methods you learned from therapy to other aspects of your life?

9 FAMILY AND FRIENDS

What Do Your Family and Friends Need to Know about Trauma Therapy?

You may have heard from friends, family and others that you should just "get over" your difficulties; that the abuse happened years ago, so you should just forget about it. Or you may have heard even worse comments that hold you responsible and blame you for the harms that were done to you.

Family and friends need to understand what triggers your traumatic responses. Without this understanding, they can reinforce the mistaken idea that you are "crazy," seriously ill or indulgent for being in therapy. The people you know may feel guilty because they weren't able to (or didn't) help or protect you. Or they may feel threatened because the healing process may have resulted in significant changes in you. For example, as you heal, you may become more assertive, more able to set boundaries and more able to talk about your needs or disappointments.

Family and friends may also be concerned for your well-being. For example, they may not understand that you could become more easily upset or frightened during different stages of healing. They may not know that people can have upsetting responses to events that happened years ago. Because of this, they may think that they are helping you by telling you to quit therapy.

The people in your life need to know that there are links between your current difficulties and the trauma you had in the past. They should understand that by dealing with the past trauma and how it affected you, you can find greater happiness and better ways to deal with the problems you are having right now.

Information for Families and Friends

Support and Understanding

Abuse in childhood usually has long-lasting harmful effects. However, healing from abuse and its traumatic impact is possible, and the support of family and friends is very important to this process. It's important to remember that women who have experienced childhood or repeated abuse are strong, and have already survived a painful and traumatic experience.

The responses and behaviours of a person who has survived long-term abuse can take a toll on everyone in the family. There are no easy solutions to these challenges. However, knowing that these problems come from the abuse experiences, and are the survivor's *normal* and understandable ways to cope with life the best she can, helps lessen some of the stress and worry that family and friends may feel.

People with post-traumatic stress often have other problems that make treatment even more complicated. For example, many people with post-traumatic stress also have substance use problems. To numb the pain of the trauma, the survivor may use alcohol or other drugs. Clinical depression is common among women with post-traumatic stress. Many abuse survivors also have chronic physical problems.

Many daily events can trigger survivors' memories of abuse (flashbacks). They may respond by "spacing out" (dissociating), withdrawing emotionally or becoming frightened or angry. Survivors may at times feel intense sadness.

Participating in family activities may become difficult or impossible. Survivors often do not want to participate in social activities. People with post-traumatic stress can withdraw from the world. They may not be interested in people and activities that were once important to them. They may lose their faith or spirituality. Partners and family members may feel helpless, not knowing how to make the person feel better.

A survivor may be unable to be employed at a job during a crisis, and that economic loss can be difficult for the family. A woman who has experienced repeated childhood or long-term adult abuse may be quick to become angry and hard to calm down. She may have trouble trusting people, including family members and people with power, such as therapists.

The support and understanding of family and friends while a survivor deals with the effects of abuse on her life can be an essential source of healing. The help of family and friends is very important to a person in trauma therapy.

COMMON EMOTIONAL REACTIONS

It is important to understand the complex and sometimes intense emotional reactions many abuse survivors may have.

The angry outbursts and mistrustful thinking that your friend or partner may have towards you, or towards others, are often more extreme because of the abuse she has been through. For example, if you hurt your partner's feelings, you may find her reaction is angrier than you think it should be. On the other hand, if you are angry with your partner, you may find that she becomes intensely anxious and fearful.

Many partners or friends of survivors respond to these extreme negative reactions by saying things like, "You're angry because of what happened to you in childhood, so don't take it out on me." This kind of response may contain some truth, but you are telling her that her current experience of being hurt isn't real. It is more likely that you did *hurt* her, but she responded as if you were *abusing* her. The problem is that one of the effects of psychological trauma is high levels of emotional arousal. This means your partner is conditioned to have intense emotional responses—automatically.

In therapy, your partner will learn techniques and methods that will help her regulate her emotional responses and separate the past from the present. She will learn that when someone is angry it does not mean that that it will lead to violence, and that when someone hurts her feelings it is not an effort to humiliate her. In the meantime, if your partner has an intense outburst because of something you said or did, admit that you hurt her and apologize.

It is important to be supportive and in control of your own reactions to your partner's intense outbursts. Do not reject or criticize her for her reactions. This can interfere with her progress and cause a setback in therapy. If you feel critical about how your partner has survived the abuse, you need to learn more about trauma therapy and talk to a professional about how you feel.

It is important for family and friends to listen with support and empathy, and to let the person in therapy talk about her feelings and reactions. Family and friends should *not* think they need to solve her problems or offer advice. It is most helpful to be able to listen.

HOW YOU CAN HELP

Take care of yourself and get support for yourself from others. Get as much information as you can about trauma and its effects. Read or talk to a professional to gain a better understanding of the survivor's reactions.

Ask your family member or friend what you can do to be helpful, and then really try to do it. Everyone's response to trauma is different and their needs are different. Don't assume you know better than the survivor does about what she needs.

Don't try to solve the person's problems or make her feelings go away. The survivor is likely to think you are uncomfortable and can't deal with her struggle. She may try to hide her feelings, which may create more distance in your relationship.

You can help the abuse survivor in the following ways:

- Whenever you can, just listen.
- Attend therapy with your partner.
- Respect her right to talk or not to talk about her feelings and past experiences of abuse.
- Understand that your partner will not always be emotionally available to you.
- Learn what makes your partner upset and ask what you can do to be helpful.
- Be clear about your availability. For example, are you available in the middle of the night if your partner or friend needs support?

- Set boundaries and limits so that you don't become resentful or burned out. You need to decide when you are available to talk and for how long. You need to communicate these limits respectfully.
- Have realistic expectations about how your partner or family member will heal. While she will learn ways to deal with her trauma responses, she may continue to have nightmares, anxiety attacks, suicidal feelings and the desire to use alcohol or other drugs.
- Try to be patient. Healing from trauma takes time.

10 GETTING ACCESS TO SERVICES

Finding suitable treatment may take some time, effort and patience.

Barriers—and Solutions— to Finding the Right Treatment

Many free services have long waiting lists.
Get on several waiting lists at once, and ask if they can call you at the last minute if someone cancels. Keep checking to find out where you are on the list.

Private therapists can be expensive.
Find out if they have a sliding scale or if they can hold some spots for lower-income clients. Private insurance does cover some costs if the therapist is a registered psychologist.

Many mental health providers do not have the specialized training needed to help women deal with the effects of trauma.
This is particularly true in rural settings, but can also be the case in large cities. Find out if the therapist has been specially trained in providing trauma treatment.

Services in languages other than English are scarce, as are services sensitive to diverse cultures.
Find out if the agency has cultural interpreters, or bring someone along who can interpret.

You do not have anyone to care for your children while you are at your appointment.
Find out if child care is offered by the service or therapist you are visiting, or whether it is okay to bring your children with you.

Who to Call to Find Trauma Therapy

The following places may be able to refer you to trained professionals who are skilled in trauma therapy:

- women's health centres
- community health centres
- therapists in private practice (including psychologists, psychiatrists and social workers)
- sexual assault centres
- women abuse crisis lines
- YWCA
- women's shelters
- spiritual centres
- family service agencies
- family physicians.

11 THE STRENGTH OF SURVIVORS

Healing from trauma takes a lot of strength, courage and determination. With the help of a therapist and new skills, you will be able to connect with others and more fully participate in life.

One woman who is a survivor of childhood abuse, and who has worked to heal from the trauma in her life, eloquently describes her process:

> *I knew the anxiety would come, and come in waves. I knew to get in a quiet place, lie down, meditate and guide the fear and shaking out of my body and watch it go. I knew to visually walk the path, in my mind's eyes, to a safe picture of calm until those painful memory pictures faded away. I knew to harness the power and channel the energy to embrace happiness for today. Hot baths, cool showers, long walks and never blaming myself are all ingredients that make up the recipe for hope in recovery from trauma from abuse.*

Healing requires support from both family and friends. It will be difficult and it will take time. Often, family and friends need more information so that they can give you support. This guide can help you and your family and friends understand how therapy can be useful to you.

The effects of trauma are debilitating, even at times life-threatening. The power the symptoms of trauma have over a person seems overwhelming. But harnessing that power can become liberating. The rewards are a full life empowered by overcoming that adversity.

SUGGESTED READINGS

BOOKS FOR THE PUBLIC

Allen, Jon G. (1995). *Coping with Trauma: A Guide to Self-Understanding.* Washington, D.C.: American Psychiatric Press.

This comprehensive book is written in plain language and explains the effects of severe trauma, and how best to cope with its symptoms and after-effects.

Cameron, Grant (1994). *What about Me? A Guide for Men Helping Female Partners Deal with Childhood Sexual Abuse.* Carp, ON: Creative Bound.

This book is for partners of women who are recovering from the trauma of childhood sexual abuse. The male author writes in plain language and discusses key issues in helping female partners heal. Some of the topics addressed include understanding suicide, dealing with anger, handling nightmares and gaining trust. The key points are summarized at the end of each chapter.

Cohen, Barry M., Barnes, Mary-Michola and Rankin, Anita B. (1995). *Managing Traumatic Stress through Art: Drawing from the Center.* Baltimore, MD: Sidran Press.

Three art therapists have collaborated to produce this workbook. It is designed especially for trauma survivors and is an extremely well-liked resource. This workbook introduces inventive and creative ways to understand, manage and transform the after-effects of trauma. The workbook contains step-by-step art projects as well as writing exercises.

Copeland, Mary Ellen and Harris, Maxine. (2000). *Healing the Trauma of Abuse: A Woman's Workbook.* Oakland, CA: New Harbinger Publications.

This workbook offers skills that trauma survivors require to deal with high levels of anxiety, depression, substance abuse, flashbacks and nightmares.

Gil, Eliana. (1983). *Outgrowing the Pain: A Book for and about Adults Abused As Children*. New York: Bantam Doubleday Dell.

This book helps survivors of childhood abuse recognize the connection between their past abuse and current struggles. The book includes questions that can help survivors recognize destructive patterns and suggestions for new ways of coping.

Matsakis, A. (1998). *Trust after Trauma: A Guide to Relationships for Survivors and Those Who Love Them*. Oakland, CA: New Harbinger.

This book is written for abuse survivors who are able to start the work of strengthening existing relationships and developing new connections in their lives. The author includes detailed exercises to help readers in healing through strengthened relationships.

Napier, Nancy J. (1993). *Getting through the Day: Strategies for Adults Hurt As Children*. New York: W.W. Norton

This book is written in straightforward language and includes an important discussion about the continuum of dissociation and the difference between ordinary mood shifts and trauma-induced dissociation. Chapters deal with triggers, mindfulness, "inner child" parts, shame, "future" self, and relationships with family, friends and therapist.

Rosenbloom, Dena and Williams, Mary Beth, with Watkins, Barbara E. (1999). *Life after Trauma: A Workbook for Healing*. New York: Guilford Press.

This workbook helps guide trauma survivors in the day-to-day process of healing. The authors include clinically proven activities, relaxation techniques, self-evaluation questionnaires and practical exercises to demonstrate how to develop effective coping and self-care strategies.

Shapiro, Francine and Forrest, Margot Silk. (1998). *EMDR: The Breakthrough Therapy for Overcoming Anxiety, Stress, and Trauma*. New York: Basic Books.

This book written for general audiences explains how EMDR works, and how it can help people who feel stuck in negative reactions and behaviours. Interspersed through the text are a variety of compelling case studies.

Vermilyea, Elizabeth. (2000). *Growing beyond Survival: A Self-Help Toolkit for Managing Traumatic Stress*. Baltimore. MD: The Sidran Press.

Growing beyond Survival is a workbook developed to help trauma survivors learn and practise skills for managing their trauma-related responses. This workbook can be used independently, as a resource in individual therapy or as part of group therapy.

Williams, Mary Beth and Poijula, Soili (2002). *The PTSD Workbook: Simple, Effective Techniques for Overcoming Traumatic Stress Symptoms*. Oakland, CA: New Harbinger Publications.

In this workbook, two psychologists gather together techniques and interventions used by post-traumatic stress experts from around the world. Readers determine the type of trauma they experienced, identify their symptoms and learn the most effective techniques and interventions they can use to overcome them.

Books and Articles for Professionals

Chu, J.A. (1998). *Rebuilding Shattered Lives.* New York: John Wiley.

Courtios, C.A. (1999). *Recollections of Sexual Abuse: Treatment Principles and Guidelines.* New York: W.W. Norton.

Dayton, Tina (2000). *Trauma and Addiction.* Deerfield Beach, FL: Health Communications Inc.

Haskell, Lori (2003). *First Stage Trauma Treatment: A Guide for Mental Health Professionals Working with Women.* Toronto: Centre for Addiction and Mental Health.

Herman, J. (1992). *Trauma and Recovery: The Aftermath of Violence—From Domestic Abuse to Political Terror.* New York: Basic Books.

Ogden, P. & Minton, K. (2000). Sensorimotor Psychotherapy: One method for processing traumatic memory. *Traumatology, VI* (3).

GLOSSARY

Attachment describes an emotional connection to another person.

Body-psychotherapy is a form of therapy that deals with the body's reactions to trauma.

Boundaries are how you define your personal space and limits, and let others know how to relate to you.

Cognitive-behavioural therapy is a type of therapy that uses many different methods, including cognitive techniques (which address how you think and deal with information) and behaviour techniques (which address your reactions to trauma).

Collaborative alliance: A way of working in which the therapist and the client work together in a partnership, to direct the healing work.

Complex post-traumatic stress describes the adaptations in psychological functioning that result from prolonged or repeated abuse or neglect. These changes in psychological functioning are diverse and can involve changes in personality, physiology, relationships and identity.

Depression is a mood disorder. It is usually diagnosed when a person has a sad, despairing mood that lasts more than two weeks and affects the person's work, school and social relationships.

Dissociation: A change in one's perception or experience of oneself and/or the external world. A feeling of "spacing out" or daydreaming.

Dual relationship: If a therapist is a client's friend, socializes with a client or provides any other service to the client (e.g., as a medical doctor), this is called a dual relationship. It is to be avoided.

Eating disorders, such as anorexia, bulimia and binge eating, are problems in which a person has extreme emotions, attitudes and behaviours toward weight and food issues.

Exposure therapy is a type of therapy in which a person is gradually exposed to a feared situation until she or he no longer has any fear of the experience.

Eye movement desensitization reprocessing (EMDR) is a type of therapy that helps people who have traumatic memories that the brain was not able to process during the traumatic event. EMDR helps the brain go back and process these memories in a safe way using eye movements, hand taps or audio tones.

Flashback: a sudden, disruptive and vivid re-experiencing of a traumatic event.

Guided imagery: While the client is in a relaxed state, he or she is asked to use imagination and mental visualization in various ways, often to increase relaxation and reduce anxiety.

Hypnotherapy: Hypnotherapy is a therapy technique using hypnosis or guided imagery. Clients learn to use mental imagery to help them change ways of thinking, feeling or behaving or to gain insight into problems.

Post-traumatic stress: a condition of experiencing the effects of a traumatic event, long after the event is over.

Psychoeducation teaches about different psychological processes and how they affect people. Psychoeducation in trauma therapy may include information about the effects of trauma in both the short-term and long-term; information about how trauma can affect the body, emotions and development; and information about abuse and neglect.

Sensorimotor psychotherapy is a type of body-psychotherapy that helps trauma survivors disconnect physical feelings from trauma-based emotions.

Simple post-traumatic stress is post-traumatic stress that results from a one-time incident, such as a rape or serious car accident.

Trauma therapy model: an approach to therapy for post-traumatic stress. A trauma therapy model considers the context of society, family, abuse and other life experiences as they affect a person's problems. Clients are viewed as partners in healing who share responsibility with the therapist for their own care.

Trigger: something (e.g., a sound, smell, emotion) that sets off or "triggers" a memory of the traumatic event.